COMMUNICATION FOR SOCIAL CHANGE:
A Position Paper and Conference Report

JANUARY 1999

This paper is organized into the following major sections:

	Page
Preface	3
Introduction	7
An Environment for New Thinking	11
The Process of Inquiry	29
Where Is Good Work Happening?	33
A Key Challenge: Capturing Impact	35
What's Next: Where Do We Go From Here?	41
Acknowledgments	

APPENDIX I
Highlights of Illustrative Work 45

APPENDIX II
1997 Bellagio Conference Highlights and
Declaration of Principles 51

1997 Bellagio Conference Participants 53

APPENDIX III
1998 Cape Town Conference Participants 54

1

COMMUNICATION FOR SOCIAL CHANGE:
A POSITION PAPER AND CONFERENCE REPORT

PREFACE

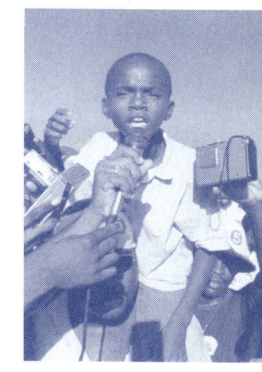

Nearly three years ago, we in the communications department of the Rockefeller Foundation began to discuss ways in which communications support for our grantees and their work can be made more effective. We were aware of the Foundation's success—and that of many other similar organizations—in bringing public attention to critical social issues. In some cases it was the result of concentrated publicity efforts and shrewd media placements. In other cases, the "newness" of the work itself —the research grants or the technological discoveries, for example—generated public interest.

We also, using strategic communications methodology, were able to continue to help grantee organizations "tell their stories" in ways that helped their policy, research or community-engagement agendas.

But it didn't seem to be enough. The true power of communication—to give people the confidence and conviction to both own the process and the content of communication in their communities—was not being sustained and, far too often, was just not thought of at all. In some ways, communication was akin to tax accounting. People and organizations thought about doing it just in time for the filing deadline. Yet for the remainder of the year, it remained a thought pushed way back into the recesses of their consciousness.

For me, with a 20-plus year career in writing, journalism, audio-visual production, public relations, corporate communications and philanthropy, this just isn't good enough. I believe that there can and should be a better way. So we set about trying to find that way. We asked a lot of smart people from around the world to join our network of inquiry.

This paper describes one way of approaching the next phase of communication for a cause. Our thinking has been influenced greatly by those who have come before us and the fields they've pioneered: social marketing, public and community relations, development communications and strategic communications.

The ideas expressed in this paper and the inquiries we're undertaking as a result of my early questions reflect an approach that we've found works well on multiple levels—from a rural village of sub-Saharan Africa to an urban neighborhood of New York City. The work that we're undertaking has at its roots the interests, desires and abilities of the people who are the recipients of the communications; the same people who should control the form and content of the communication processes.

To our delight, we've discovered the coalescing power of this inquiry. We've found in the past months that virtually everyone we talk to—from activists to community and non-governmental organization (NGO) leaders to policymakers, academics, business leaders and other foundation executives—has a similar reaction: "great— I'd like to know more." Such responses motivate us and fuel our enthusiasm.

We're using the phrase *communication for social change* as a convenient way of thinking and organizing. This work is based on a simple assumption: that we can indeed find effective ways to use the discipline of communication to make a greater contribution to the pace of development. For we know that when communication is a full partner in the development process and is executed intelligently, the progress of development is more sustainable. We also believe that a lot of evangelizing must be done in order to help communication become such a full partner.

The purpose of this position paper is to update the reader on the communication for social change work, and to report the findings of a Rockefeller Foundation sponsored conference on the subject held in Cape Town, South Africa, in October 1998. The predominant thinking behind this paper and of the conference is the basis of the communication for social change philosophy.

The paper, written by me and James Deane of the Panos Institute, is meant to be thought-provoking and a discussion starter. We realize that we have more questions than answers—and that in some areas there simply are no answers. But we do hope we have adequately outlined the salient issues and proposed a few innovative ideas that can be adapted and transmitted throughout communities in the world. We look forward to your response.

Denise Gray-Felder
The Rockefeller Foundation

PREFACE

INTRODUCTION

This paper is a status report on an evolving field known as communication for social change. The ideas expressed here are a compilation of inputs from a network of professionals across the world which the Rockefeller Foundation's department of communications has assembled to help us explore new ideas and test innovative communication concepts.

Communication for social change is part of an evolution of communications methodology that can help accelerate global development. The process began in the first quarter of the 20th century with the use of publicity tools to bring attention to social problems such as

hunger and disease. It grew to a reliance on public relations as a means of identifying stakeholders and creating programs to fit the audience's interests. More recently, social marketing took center stage—where sophisticated marketing and cause-related advertising tools were applied to influence individual and societal behaviors—such as convincing couples in poor nations to use contraceptives. This was followed by development communications and strategic communications, the latter which rightfully considers communication to be a process rather than as a series of products.

In the pages that follow, the two authors argue that communication for social change is a distinct way of doing communications—and one of the few approaches that can be sustained. Such sustainability is largely due to the fact that ownership of both the message and the medium—the content and the process—resides with the individuals or communities affected.

We believe that this approach can help make greater contributions to the pace of development. From this basic assumption we move to questioning "how" and "if" and "where" we might find interesting work and committed individuals to test the effectiveness of this approach.

In order to do this work, the Rockefeller Foundation has brought together a group of social activists, academics, filmmakers and journalists, funders, electronic communications experts, service providers, and professional communicators. The ideas expressed in this position paper reflect discussions held at two conferences – one at the foundation's Bellagio Study and Conference Center on Lake Como, in Italy, and the other in the fall of 1998 in Cape Town, South Africa.

In Bellagio we committed to a new agenda for global communications: communication that is empowering, many-to-many (horizontal versus top-down), communication that gives voice to the previously unheard, and that has a bias toward local content and ownership. The group's action steps, agreed upon at the end of the meeting, include a commitment to convince others of the value of this approach (broadening the debate), to publicize writings about the effectiveness of this work, and to continue to study the prospects in a global setting. During the Cape Town gathering, we continued the inquiry with an expanded group of people. There we developed a concrete and comprehensive definition of communication for social change, put together an outline for the skills and attributes needed to do this work, began work on the skills/resources training "toolbox" or "practitioner's kit" or "knowledge transfer," reached agreement on measurements, and identified organizations and people that we'd like to engage in helping us do this work and to advocate for its effectiveness.

What follows is further explanation of the value and benefits of the discipline of communication for social change.

An Environment for New Thinking

THE PREMISE

This initiative is based on a simple premise: that recent developments—in communications technologies, in political and media systems, and in emerging development problems—suggest a greatly enhanced, radically different role for communication in development programming.

Communication programming has, very simplistically, tended to fulfill three roles in development thinking and practice:

First, its role has been to inform and persuade people to adopt certain behaviors and practices that are beneficial to them: for example, to inform people how to protect themselves from HIV and to persuade them to use a condom; to persuade them of the importance of vaccinating their child and to inform them when and where they can do so; to persuade them that simple sugar and salt solutions can cure diarrhea and to inform them how to make them up; to persuade them to have fewer children and to inform them how to do so.

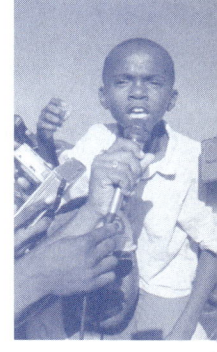

Second, it has been used to enhance the image and profile of the work of organizations involved in development with a view to boosting the credibility of their

11

work, raising more funding and generally improving public perceptions.

Third, it has been used on a more targeted level within communities to enable community consultation over specific initiatives.

The communication for social change initiative believes that all these roles are important and communication work in general remains underfunded and undervalued. We argue that these traditional approaches to communication are generally insufficient in addressing the reality of the development problems that exist, and they do not always reflect the complex changes in the communications environments taking place in many developing country societies.

We argue in this position paper that communication can play a much greater role in enabling people to take control over their own lives, in enabling people and societies to set their own agendas in relation to political, economic and social development; and in enabling, in particular, the voices of the economically and politically marginalized to be amplified and channeled to mainstream public and political debate.

We argue that the interaction between communication and the social well-being of people in developing countries will be radically redefined over the next few years. Global economic liberalization of communications, the deployment of the Internet, mobile telephony and other new technologies, and the changing political environment in most developing countries are all coinciding to make the cusp of the new millennium a defining moment which will determine how successfully all countries, especially developing nations, adapt to and exploit these changes.

Information in society does not simply enable people to know what they should do or think. Information is power—it enables people to make sense of their lives and it enables them to shape their aspirations. Ultimately it can enable them to take control of their lives. In many areas of the world, people have precious little access to information outside their community that enables them to make such "sense."

In other societies, despite a multitude of information outlets, people who are historically marginalized and excluded remain "voiceless" and "invisible" because those who control information channels refuse to share access equitably. Communication for social change principles focus on using direct, many-to-many communications which spring from the affected communities.

The problems inherent in this work are those which have plagued communication practice for decades: how to assess impact beyond counting products produced or net impressions received; how to program communication for social change work on the micro community level and on the macro multinational level, often simultaneously; and how to transfer knowledge and skills to those most in need of "training" who often live and work in hard-to-reach areas. We also struggle with ways to capture the best learning—those cases that illustrate the power of communication for social change, yet are not overly simplistic.

Language is also a challenge: the notion of how to explain this work in terms that can be readily accessible and used by grassroots activists as easily as by professional communicators.

These are all issues that the groups assembled for the Rockefeller Foundation conferences grappled with. This paper reveals some preliminary thoughts on solutions. Others, such as site-based knowledge transfer, are in the early exploratory stages and will require more study, testing and applications, especially in developing nations with scarce human and financial resources.

Yet nothing in our questions should suggest lack of conviction nor should they prevent us from energetically embracing the potential of communication for social change to fulfill critical gaps in the development process.

WHAT IS COMMUNICATION FOR SOCIAL CHANGE?

The traditional understanding of the role of communication in development is one that seeks mainly to change individual behaviors. This behavior-change communication can be broadly defined as a process of understanding people's situations and influences, developing messages that respond to the concerns within those situations, and using communication processes and media to persuade people to increase their knowledge and change the behaviors and practices that place them at risk.

Communication for social change, on the other hand, is defined as a process of public and private dialogue through which people define who they are, what they want and how they can get it. Social change is defined as change in people's lives as they themselves define such change. This work seeks particularly to improve the lives of the politically and economically marginalized, and is informed by principles of tolerance, self-determination, equity, social justice and active participation for all.

This approach attempts to rebalance strategic approaches to communication and change by taking the overriding emphasis:

- Away from people as the objects for change … and on to people and communities as the agents of their own change;
- Away from designing, testing and delivering messages … and on to supporting dialogue and debate on the key issues of concern;
- Away from the conveying of information from technical experts … and on to sensitively placing that information into the dialogue and debate;
- Away from a focus on individual behaviors … and on to social norms, policies, culture and a supportive environment;
- Away from persuading people to do something … and on to negotiating the best way forward in a partnership process;
- Away from technical experts in "outside" agencies dominating and guiding the process … and on to the people most affected by the issues of concern playing a central role.

The Starting Point:
A Changed Communications Environment...

The starting point for this inquiry is the growing evidence that, as a generality, the "communications environment" in which most people on the planet live has changed radically over the last decade. It has changed both in relation to the information people have access to, and the opportunities people have to communicate their own perspectives on issues that concern them.

This new communications environment is shaped by three main interlocking trends:

I. Media liberalization and deregulation,

II. New information and communication technologies,

III. The changing global political and economic context.

In general, and with important exceptions, these trends are tending to decentralize communications in developing countries, with a trend towards a more fragmented, more horizontal, people-to-people model of communication, and away from a highly centralized, vertical model.

In industrialized countries, media liberalization suggests more choice for consumers, which should, theoretically, mean increased access. Yet the way it plays out in countries like the United States is in encouraging the growth of huge media monopolies that result in far less community input to programming. With deregulation, public-service programming has become just a fading memory, and station ownership has leaped beyond the realm of possibility for most community-based organizations or individuals of color.

This new communications environment has, we argue, important implications for development programming, an importance that is compounded by the emergence of new development problems—such as HIV/AIDS—that demand new approaches to communication. Our inquiry suggests that there are many opportunities to be seized, as well as real challenges to be faced in understanding and acting upon these changes.

I. The Changing Media: Media Liberalization and Deregulation

Most people on this planet receive most of their information on issues beyond their immediate communities from the print and broadcast media.

Fifteen years ago, much of humanity had one main source for this information—their governments. The means were stolid, formulaic broadcast and print media that had been established with the express purpose of telling people what they should know and think.

Two general trends have changed this. First, following the end of the Cold War, a combination of internal pressure from their citizens and external pressure—often in the form of conditions set by donors—have led governments to relax censorship and freedom of speech laws. Second, this pressure for political liberalization has been combined with economic liberalization and deregulation of national media industries.

The result in many of those countries with tightly controlled media has been a blossoming of dynamic, generally populist and highly commercial newspapers, television and radio media in most developing countries, and flourishing of new community media in some. Meanwhile, old monopoly state-run media, particularly broadcasters, have tended to languish, losing their audiences to more dynamic competition. They also face declining government support and funding.

The implications of these changes for those involved in communication are challenging. Monopoly broadcasters have presented a convenient way of communicating simple messages to huge audiences through one medium. In much more fragmented media environments, this opportunity no longer exists and reaching the same audience requires putting messages out through many different media, and adapting it to many different audiences.

Perhaps more importantly, the creation of these more complex and dynamic communications environments raises the deeper question of just what information do people have access to, and does it empower poor people and give them a greater voice—or does it move them further to the economic and social margins?

At their worse, new communications environments have done the latter. They have shifted from providing stodgy and dogmatic government propaganda to providing a uniform diet of often Western popular music. In some countries, state-controlled news has been replaced by no news, or information that is sensational, inaccurate or irrelevant to the daily lives of much of its audience, or news that is derived entirely from international sources. Often operating in anarchic regulatory environments, commercial and private stations have little obligation to provide anything other than entertainment. At their very worst, media have encouraged intolerance, sectionalism and tribalism, the most extreme example being the "hate" radio of RTML in Rwanda which played a key role in the massacres in that country.

At their best, however, commercial, community and, in some cases, newly invigorated state-run news and media organizations have managed to attract large audiences with compelling, popular and informative programming. In Kampala, Uganda, the FM station Capital Radio attracts some of its highest audiences for its Capital Doctor program, which provides advice and information on issues of sex, HIV/AIDS and other health issues. In South Africa, a form of "edutainment"—"Soul City," set in a Johannesburg township—has become one of the most popular soap operas in the country, yet has succeeded in educating people about diarrhea, HIV/AIDS and other issues.

Again in South Africa, deregulation has spurred the creation of more than 80 community radio stations broadcasting in 15 languages. Community stations have made serious inroads into the broadcast markets, often stealing audiences from the well-established public broadcasting stations. Community broadcasting provides communities with information that is relevant to their lives, as well as a voice through which people can make demands. In Cape Town, the tiny community radio station, Radio Zibonele, drew on their audience's anger to play a key role in mediating and resolving the township's gang warfare surrounding the taxi business. (See Appendix I for more detail.)

In fact, the success of community radio proves, in some small way, the ready market for communication for social change principles to be applied in diverse circumstances throughout the world. In addition to sub-Saharan African nations, community radio has succeeded where little else can from northwest Canada to Southeast Asia.

The print media too is changing under similar pressure, with more entertaining, more populist and often more trenchant coverage of news issues. These changes have demonstrated how, in the print media in particular, poor reporting undermines many other forms of social and political discourse; high-quality reporting can play a major role in promoting and stimulating constructive public debate. Well-informed, investigative reporting in particular can provide a key element of public accountability, both for national governments, for international institutions, and for NGOs and other civil-society organizations.

Finally, the last decade has seen an explosion in satellite broadcasting. Take the south Asia region, home to one-fifth of the world's population which is today within the footprint of at least 50 broadcast satellites. In India, Pakistan and Bangladesh alone there are more than 70 million households with television sets, adding up to a total viewership of 300 million. By 2007, there will be 550 million television viewers in these countries. Half of them will be hooked up to cable—able to watch the 350 channels that will be available to them by then.

These changes do not apply to all people in all countries, but in one form or another they do affect the vast majority of people in the great majority of countries. They present many problems; reaching lots of people with prepared messages is becoming more difficult and more expensive. They also present substantial opportunities: to work with communities to enable them to amplify their voices, to enable access to the information that can empower them, to help shape communication environments that can work for people, not against them.

II. New Information and Communication Technologies

The current revolution in information technologies represents probably the most profound set of technological developments human society has experienced since the industrial revolution. The innovations of the Internet—and particularly e-mail—have transformed communications capacities in countries with often dilapidated telecommunications infrastructures; and have opened up access to much more information about global issues. The falling costs and increased access to telephony mean that an increasing number of people have the capacity to communicate rapidly beyond their immediate communities, thus opening up new economic opportunities and opportunities for social and political discourse.

For many participants in this communication for social change initiative these technologies represent a huge opportunity:

- Centralized control of information by governments or commercial interests becomes much more difficult. Increasingly, political systems can neither control the information their citizens receive nor monitor or constrain how they communicate with each other. Technology is—for good and ill—increasing access to the kind of information that is uncensored and unfiltered. Technology is growing most rapidly in those areas where its demand is most clearly defined by the users.

- The capacity of people to access information is substantially increased.

- The capacity of people to organize, advocate and lobby beyond physical boundaries is greatly enhanced.

- The capacity for people and organizations in developing countries to communicate information—their aspirations, demands, experiences, analysis—becomes cheaper, more powerful and far more pervasive.

Nevertheless, we also recognize the limitations of these technologies. In particular, the "information gap" between rich and poor is stark. One of the least expensive of the information and communications technologies (ICTs)—the telephone—illustrates just how far apart the rich and poor worlds are in access to such technologies. One quarter of the countries in the world still have fewer than one telephone line per 100 people. The

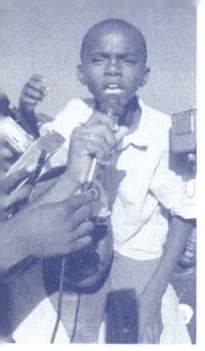

majority of the population in developing countries—60 percent of the total—live in rural areas. Yet in these countries, more than 80-percent of main telephone lines are in urban areas.[1] The distribution of new ICTs is no more equal. Eighty-four percent of mobile cellular subscribers, 91 percent of all fax machines and 97 percent of Internet host computers are in developed countries.

Telecommunications are nevertheless becoming cheaper, more reliable and more accessible and will continue to do so. Despite the constraints, it seems likely that we are seeing the emergence internationally of organizational structures that are increasingly based on networks, rather than hierarchies. It is this revolution which represents most powerfully the increase in horizontal, people-to-people communication, and which provides profound new opportunities for more inclusive public and policy debate.

III. A Changing Political and Economic Environment

The collapse of the Soviet Union and the end of the Cold War have had far-reaching effects, a full exploration of which is beyond the remit of this paper. However, two key issues should be mentioned.

The first is the growing, though uneven, democratization and political liberalization that has swept much of the developing world over the last decade. Many of the highly centralized one-party states or dictatorships have given way to multiparty democracies, or at least to more open political systems.

[1] All figures taken from *World Telecommunication Development Report*, International Telecommunication Union (ITU), 1998.

Secondly, this political liberalization has been matched by a still more pervasive economic liberalization. We have seen the rapid emergence of a new global economy. As Manuel Castells argues, "for the first time in human history the entire planet is capitalist, since even the few remaining command economies are surviving or developing through their linkages to global, capitalist markets." As all governments are finding, including China's, maintaining strict and centralized control of information in a market economy (which, in turn, needs to rely on communications technologies) is both difficult and often inefficient.

The fragmentation and decentralization of information outlined above is potentially countered by the greater concentration of ownership in communications and media industries ushered in by globalization. According to UNESCO's World Communication Report 1997, "international [media] conglomerates are emerging with the purpose of controlling not only the transmission system (manufacturing, network, cable, satellite, etc.) but also the programs they convey." An increasing spate of mergers and acquisitions over recent years has seen the emergence of a handful of "world companies" who now dominate global media markets. Time Warner Inc., News International, Sony, Finivest and Bertelsman each have annual sales well in excess of $10 billion, an increasing percentage of which is generated outside the United States. This concentration is compounded by convergence of media and telecommunications industries leading to still greater concentration of ownership.

Such concentration may not matter and may be offset by the more horizontal and decentralized models of communications outlined above. But both these trends—towards a decentralization of information production away from government, and a concentration of ownership of the means of communication in the hands of transnationals—should matter to anyone involved in communication. These trends are bound up intimately with questions of who controls the information that people receive.

Communication and Emerging Development Problems

These changes to communication environments come at the same time as important changes in how we think about development. Some of the most important emerging development challenges of the last decade have raised new questions.

Issues such as HIV/AIDS, reproductive health and reproductive rights, and others such as tobacco use have highlighted more intensely than ever how disease and poor health are linked not only to poverty and poor nutrition, but also to prejudice, to social, political and economic inequality, and to social dislocation. They have focused an especially strong spotlight on social and political environments where issues of sex and sexuality are habitually hidden or are difficult to debate in public.

Such complexities are forcing societies globally to change—to question long-cherished, deeply rooted social, political and religious mores and practices. A

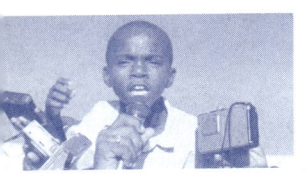

whole range of issues—from HIV to reproductive rights, from domestic violence to female genital mutilation—have crystallized the need for much wider social and political change. Such change is informed by what happens both within countries and by international debates, but if it is to be sustainable, change has to emerge from within societies.

The means of how societies change, and who drives such change is contentious and difficult. Part of such change will come from education about issues such as condom use—but much of the more deep-seated changes that need to take place in societies, such as the improvement in the status of women, need to emerge from advocacy and vigorous public debate within and between societies.

Such debates depend fundamentally on communication: on communication within societies, within families, within communities, through political discourse; and on communication between societies, at the levels of the individual, of the community and of the global society. The capacity of people to communicate is intimately bound up with their capacity to effect change.

In short, a new model of communication could be emerging from a mixture of political, technological, economic and social change. It is decentralized, pluralistic and democratic; it seeks to empower rather than persuade people; it fosters debate among and between citizens, among and between communities, and between people and government. This model envisages increasingly horizontal communication allowing people to communicate with each other easily and inexpensively. It also involves the steady disintegration of traditional monolithic vertical lines of communication, where governments owned radio and television stations in order to control flows of information.

The Upshot: Creating an Environment for Change

The Rockefeller Foundation has responded to a growing body of opinion and evidence that the role of communication in developing-country societies is changing, and that the strategies of those working in development needed to change with it. The Foundation's inquiry is based on the premise that the changes which are taking place in communication and society may have profound implications for donor and development strategies, but that this premise remains poorly researched and articulated.

Communication for social change programming suggests a major shift in development. Above all it is about enabling publics and communities to articulate their own agendas for development—at the community, the provincial, the national and the international level.

Programming in this area is about making connections—at these different levels and between them. It involves making connections between global trade policies and local communities, and it involves making connections between many different kinds of activities—between the issues themselves (such as HIV/AIDS, domestic violence) and the means that exist for debating and discussing them: community radio, women's radio listeners groups, an informed and responsive national media, quality media programming (e.g., Soul City), telecommunications.

It involves framing and phrasing debates in language and forms that are inclusive. It involves a responsibility of academics in particular, but those concerned with development in general, to communicate research and information not only to their peers, but to the wider public within developing countries. It involves "returning" research and analysis to where it originates.

Perhaps, above all, it suggests that the key role for donor and development institutions is to create an environment for change. It suggests a role that sees these organizations continuing to inform and create development strategies, but also in creating the conditions where developing-country societies can assess, challenge and adapt such strategies and begin to create strategies for themselves.

It provides new opportunities to open up development decisions and programming to public debate and dialogue, and to enable publics—and not just experts—to be more proactive in shaping debate on development issues.

The Process of Inquiry

The Rockefeller Foundation has been engaged aggressively in intellectual inquiry about the power of communications for nearly 60 years. In the late 1930s, program officer John Marshall formed the Rockefeller Communications Seminar whose goal was to promote a theoretical framework about the role of mass communications in American culture. Under Marshall's guidance, the foundation funded one of the country's first efforts to quantitatively document the effect of radio on listeners. The work expanded in the 1940s to include support for Paul Lazarsfeld, who began the new field of communication and attitude research. In this time frame, the Foundation also funded the creation of the first communications journal, Public Opinion Quarterly.

It is from this historical base that the current communications efforts to promote an enhanced discipline known as communication for social change grows. The Rockefeller Foundation, like most other progressive U.S.-based foundations, is in the business of positive social change—change in attitudes, in behaviors, in utilization of technology, and of access to opportunities to enhance lives. While a key player in the development arena, the Foundation's focus remains predominantly on science-based knowledge. Yet at the core of much of the Foundation's current portfolio is the need to affect individual and community norms and behaviors—the type of change that requires sophisticated, sustained communication.

Three years ago we began to ask the tough questions: how can we demonstrate that communication—planned and implemented strategically—can indeed bring about desired social change? Can we prove that such communication thinking and work is as systematic, scientific, sustained and measurable as other social sciences? And can we move beyond publicity and promotional activities to a new way of thinking and delivering communication that starts with the identified community or stakeholder's needs, engages the recipient of the communication in decision making and, most importantly, can be sustained and replicated.

The answers are "yes", "maybe" and "watch us."

We began this inquiry the way much work starts at this Foundation—with a group of people coming together at a Bellagio conference. While this may not have been a unique method, the process of discovery we used—search conference methodology—yielded encouraging results. We brought together disparate types with little in common except our belief that communication MUST be done differently. We, individually and collectively, knew that we were on the cusp of an evolutionary turn in the history of communication for development. We felt that our work had to be bigger than embracing electronic technology or providing access to those in "unwired" parts of the world. We also believed, with some certainly, that the discipline of communication can be ill-defined, misunderstood, undervalued and often ignored for its contributions to the development process.

What we're about today is, hopefully, adding to the discourse rather than muddying it.

In the process of figuring out what to do and where to start, we realized that the type of communication work that needs to be done is not often done—especially in poor areas of developing nations most in need. It seems that a particular niche for this network will be in identifying needed skills, developing ways to transmit training and reaching those people and communities most likely to have scarce resources. Going forward we will work with such people and communities to bring communication for social change to them.

We come to this work humbly confident that ultimately, development—in virtually any sector—cannot happen without innovative and sustained communication processes.

THE PROCESS OF INQUIRY

Where Is Good Work Happening?

Questions that we're asked frequently are "what does communication for social change look like? Who is practicing it, or where is the greatest potential?"

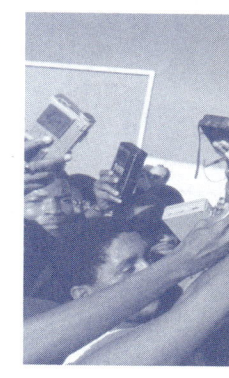

In looking for examples of good work, it's important to keep in mind the key principles of communication for social change: it empowers individuals and communities, it engages people in making decisions that enhance their lives, it is many-to-many, it relies on democratic ideals, it allows previously unheard voices to be heard, and both the process of communications and the content of the messages are controlled by the receiving communities. This can be heady stuff—at times bordering on the ideal rather than the practical. Yet even so, we've found examples of innovative social communications work in several locales.

As we work in the United States, Africa and Asia, for example, it appears that the most likely practitioners of communication for social change are small struggling organizations with few resources. Communication for social change in some respects becomes a means of survival. Without the benefit of large communications staffs or budgets, and facing media that are hesitant to cover social issues in substantive ways, some small NGOs and community-based organizations have figured out how to use the people most affected by their work to make the communications process work.

In Africa and Latin America, the community radio movement stands out. By definition, community radio stations cannot succeed without local control, citizen participation, local issues-based programming and open access. Yet radio remains essentially a top-down methodology; that is, someone decides what will be broadcast, it airs, and is received passively by listeners. The better community radio stations, such as Cape Flats' Bush Radio (South Africa), Radio Zibonele in the Khayelitsha community of Cape Town, South Africa, and Johannesburg's Alexandra Township's community station focus on audience participation. New programming stems from the suggestions listeners make when telephoning into the stations, or when they are working there as volunteer staff. Critical issues facing the communities are discussed —and problem solving happens in real time—on the air.

Outreach is daily and continuous—the community radio stations are vital parts of the neighborhoods where they operate. They don't just "cover" issues—they lead the residents in collective decision making.

Appendix I includes excerpts from three case studies which reflect many of the principles of communication for social change.

A Key Challenge: Capturing Impact

Recognition of the role of communication in achieving social change is not necessarily new nor surprising, but it receives comparatively little funding. While the case for this kind of programming—for the reasons already given—is building, there remain significant obstacles to it attracting major support.

Much of this work involves stimulating dialogue and debate within communities and the public, and—when it works best—ensuring that the engine of change is the community and the public itself. As a consequence, much of this work is unpredictable and risky. Because dialogue and debate are the immediate objectives and are difficult to measure or attribute to any particular intervention, and because it is recognized that social change is likely to take a long time, this work is very difficult to assess and evaluate.

Indeed, many of the communications initiatives that are currently funded—particularly around behavior change—attract support less because they are perceived as addressing the main problem, but more because they can be claimed as having changed something. In the field of HIV/AIDS, for example, much of the funding for communications initiatives has gone into attempts to change individual behaviors. Much of this work has had substantial impact but it has not, as many of its practitioners would acknowledge, sought to change the underlying factors that are driving a still-escalating epidemic: poverty, social exclusion, prejudice and discrimination, migration, and poor health systems.

Such problems are fundamental. Communication for social change programming can constitute only part of the real solution; it can help enable people to shape their own agenda, articulate their own priorities and aspirations of how to address the epidemic, and ensure that donors are following and responding to public and policy debates within developing countries as well as shaping such debates.

Evaluation of impact in this area remains difficult but not, we conclude, impossible. It does, however, mean that we must develop new methodologies.

Measurements and Evaluation[2]
Why Measure Impact?

Donors have a right and an obligation to demand evidence that their funds have been spent wisely, that they have achieved what they were meant to, or that there are good reasons for any changes or lack of achievement. However, there are other reasons why impact needs to be measured.

1. Accountability—understanding the impact of communication interventions is an essential component of being accountable. The primary accountability is to the people engaged in the communication intervention. Being involved with them in aspects of their lives requires that

---

[2] *Based on writings by Warren Feek, The Communication Initiative. Feek worked with a subgroup of participants of the Cape Town conference on communication for social change to develop these concepts.*

accountability. They are also the people, proportionate to their means, who will invest the most resources.

2. Progress—understanding what is happening and whether it is what people want to happen.

3. Improvement—information from any measurement and evaluation is crucial to both large strategic decisions and to fine-tuning communication interventions in order that better value is gained from the investments that are made.

4. Motivation—a sense of achievement is crucial to motivation. Good motivation is an essential element of any endeavor, including communication for social change programs. The people involved draw energy and drive from knowing that progress is being made. Not knowing can lead to the opposite.

5. Credibility—Good data on the impact of communication for social change interventions can only enhance the credibility of this field and the investments, from local to international, that are made.

Measure What?

The long-term goal of all development action is to see positive change in the issues of concern. We all want less poverty, increased employment, better gender equality, eradication of HIV/AIDS, more girls in school, higher educational achievement, lower child- and maternal-mortality rates, better nutrition, fewer accidents, and no violence. That is the crucial measure of success. Such changes can take five years or a decade, but generally much longer. People involved in communication for social change initiatives need more immediate data that indicates whether what they are doing is making a contribution to the overall change process. It is not possible to run a program for 15 years before assessing impact and then finding that the wrong things were done. More immediate information on the contribution of communication to change is required.

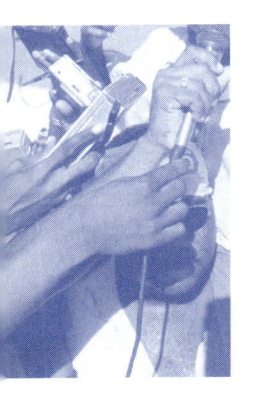

Although communication for social change activities tend to have less specific and immediate objectives and targets, they nevertheless need to develop a similar set of indicators both to measure and indicate progress and to drive the nature of the programming.

We are at the start of this work, but the Cape Town meeting, drawing on the information, analysis and perspectives above, made some suggestions of indicators:

- Expanded public and private dialogue and debate

    Dialogue and debate are crucial. They indicate that people are engaging in the issues of concern, are motivated to look at them, and that at least some of the parties to the debate and discussion are challenging the orthodoxy that may be contributing to the matters of most concern. For example, the role of women in politics, the need for a more open approach to sexual health issues, equal rights for boys and girls, and land redistribution.

- Increased accuracy of the information that people share in the dialogue/debate

Accuracy of information is important. There are two types of information. First, specific, proven data such as would exist in relation to a particular medical issue. Second, accurately reflecting the background information, perspectives and views of the parties to a debate over a more complex issue such as girls in school. The more accurately the data and the perspectives are reflected in the dialogue—from among friends to public policy debate—the more likely is the chance of positive change.

- The means available that enable people/communities to feed their voices into debate and dialogue

- Increased leadership and agenda-setting role by disadvantaged people on the issues of concern

Whatever the focus of the communication for social change action the people at the center of the issue[s] those whose everyday lives are most affected—should be involved in the major decisions related to the initiative. This will ensure relevance and meaning—a vital component for any intervention.

- Resonates with the major issues of interest to people's everyday interests

Communication for social change interventions need to be positioned in ways that resonate, make sense to them, to which they can relate. Of course this is a basic tenet of all communication, but it can be easily forgotten in the midst of complex detail relating to an issue such as breast-feeding and HIV/AIDS. If the positioning of the issue does resonate there is a greater chance of momentum and action. And it is not possible to focus on all the many and varied aspects of a concern. Rarely can the issue that resonates be chosen in advance. It will emerge and then needs to be accentuated.

- Linked people and groups with similar interests who might otherwise not be in contact

One of the main turning points for any change process is when different groups form alliances with a common overall objective and a loose coordination framework. Each group does its own thing, but in the knowledge that it contributes to a greater effort. Therefore activities that link people together and help working alliances can be interpreted as contributing to positive change.

What's Next: Where Do We Go From Here?

Throughout the NGO community in industrialized and in less-wealthy nations, the potential both to apply communication for social change methodology and to encourage its use is great. The change-communication principles seem obvious to those of us in development, philanthropy and social services. They speak to the very essence of our work—that is, to helping create locally-based solutions to critical social ills.

Yet throughout time, obvious "fixes" have been the ones most often overlooked. "Of course innovative communication techniques are essential" we hear frequently. "Of course we have to empower those 'on the ground' to have greater control of their own stories and how they are communicated. Of course 'horizontal' communication is more effective than top-down," we all opine.

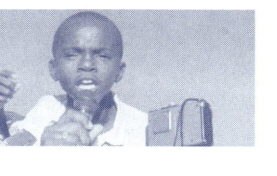

Yet "how" remains a mystery in far too many instances. Or more precisely, we're not sure "how to make it work."

Key to answering the "how" question, we believe, is in finding smart practitioners and thinkers throughout the world who are able to reach others, train others, test the change-communication principles, encourage ongoing site-based work and evaluate its effectiveness.

41

WHERE DO WE GO FROM HERE?

The strategy for moving this initiative forward has five prongs:

1. Reaching clarity of terms and defining, or perhaps refining, the field;

2. Identifying and describing the skills, attributes and resources necessary for communication for social change. During the Cape Town conference, participants discussed both the form and content of the skills-development process;

3. Developing the systems and exchange mechanisms needed to spread the change communication work globally;

4. Maintaining the network of supporters and enrolling additional supporters; and,

5. Using concrete measurements to evaluate effectivness and the reach of communication for social change.

We are well along on the first prong. We believe we have many good ideas for the second and third ones. Each day we're thrilled by another expression of interest that we receive; the word is getting out, which only fuels our evangelical spirits. And, as this paper suggests, there are different ways of doing evaluation that should further the communication for social change agenda.

Yet, many questions remain: can we create a "transfer of knowledge" or type of curriculum that can be transported worldwide easily and economically? What's in such a curriculum? Who are the trainers? How will they receive the information? (Is, for example, Internet-based training a viable option?) Can we establish regional centers of learning that are based on local realities? How do we reach people in those areas of the world most in need of this knowledge but who have the smallest number of resources to access such training?

Or should we, perhaps, be worrying less about skills and more about personal attributes?

Going forward we must debate answers to these questions and test possible solutions on a community-specific basis.

At the end of our recent Cape Town conference those attending committed to the series of actions listed below.

Defining/Refining the Field

Create a document that discusses the implications of media ownership as it relates to achieving communication for social change goals.

Skills Development/Training/Knowledge Transfer

Assess the training needs of NGOs and community-based organizations in order to make recommendations about modes of training. Explore the concept of "co-production" as a way of delivering communication for social change training.

Create a pilot "toolbox" of skills sets that can be tested in field applications. Seek partner organizations for this work.

Research, edit and publish a full body of case stories illustrative of communication for social change at work.

Learn more about how communication—as a somewhat intrusive process—creates intended and unintended consequences that must be anticipated and managed, especially in complex political environments.

Resource Exchange

Disseminate information, reports and papers about communication for social change on a regular basis in print and electronic form through global, regional and national networks.

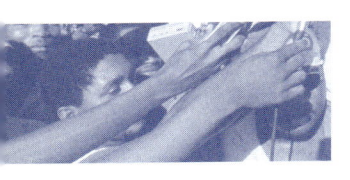

Each participant is to share widely information within his/her spheres of influence.

Maintain and expand the network of professionals supportive of change communications.

Create a repository of materials contributed by those in the network via a Web site. Use other dissemination strategies.

Measurements and Evaluation

Finish and distribute a working paper on measures and evaluation. Test the concepts in nonprofit organizations in which network members have contacts.

The road ahead looks promising. We wish to thank the 50-plus people who started this journey with us and the hundreds of others who have expressed interest in helping advance the field. We're confident that as information about the field grows, so will the number of supporters. And, that, as a result of our collective dedication to more effective communication, ultimately, the quality of life for many will be enhanced.

Acknowledgments

We acknowledge, with gratitude, that this work would not be possible without the commitment of time, talent and brainpower of the participants of both Rockefeller Foundation sponsored conferences on this subject.

Appendix I

The following three excerpts describe projects that reflect communication for social change principles. Their inclusion here does not suggest that they are fully representative of the best work in the world, but rather that their approaches have been successful.

Radio Zibonele: Khayelistsha, Cape Town, South Africa[3]

Driving on the N2 highway from the Cape Town airport, you travel over 12 kilometers alongside concrete slated fence. You glimpse small wooden structures with corrugated metal or plastic as roofs, held down by rocks. The casual observer is often unaware that more than 700,000 people live on the other side of the fence on this vast sand flat in Khayelistsha, the home of Radio Zibonele. The station went on the air illegally under South Africa's apartheid government, broadcasting health information once per week as one of the projects of a local clinic.

The station's mission statement is: "Our concern is to enhance the quality of life through improving the health standards of our people. All those we serve are affected by poor health and poor environmental conditions. Radio Zibonele is committed to sharing skills and information through honest process, hereby empowering the community of Khayelitsha for better life."

[3] Excerpted from a case study written by Bill Siemering with Jean Fairbairn and Norma Rangana of the Open Society Foundation for South Africa.

Now independent of the health clinic and its sponsor, NPPHCN Media and Training Centre, the station continues its commitment in various ways. For example:

- The station has been broadcasting 19 hours a day, five days a week since January 1, 1997.
- On a Tuesday, when Vusi Tshose, the station manager, learned of a possible school strike because of overcrowding, he called the local minister of education and mediated a meeting with the affected parties. They met on a Wednesday and Thursday, and announced the solution on the air on Friday, averting a strike.
- High-school teachers present summaries of their courses at the end of the school year for students studying for the matric standard 10 exams. Some young people from neighboring townships outside the listening area come to Khayelitsha to sleep over to hear the programs. Educators believe that the review and tips on how to take an exam have enabled more students to pass the test.
- When rival taxi groups were in dispute, involving violence and gang warfare, they were invited to come to the station, state their cases and ask the community how they wanted them to operate.

Self-help is the underlying theme of the station. A key strength is the staff's knowledge of their listeners. As one volunteer presenter said, "If there's a shot, we hear it too. If the power goes out, it goes out for us too." This intimate knowledge of the community is one of the unique advantages of community radio that cannot be matched by for-profit radio. Nearly all Radio Zibonele programming is presented in Xhosa with occasional English phrases.

According to one survey, Radio Zibonele has an audience of 105,000; nearly one-third of all listeners to community radio in the western Cape. They are able to cover their monthly operating costs (R25,000 or about U.S. $5,000) through advertising and sponsorships. But they do not accept advertising dollars from cigarette or alcohol producers as these habits are bad for the community. All this work is done with a paid staff of four and 30 volunteers working from a truck container, broadcasting with a 20-watt transmitter.

EcoNews: Information for Decision Making Within an African Context[4]
The Community Media Program

EcoNews Africa is a NGO initiative that analyzes global environment and development issues from an African perspective, and reports on local, national and regional activities that contribute to global solutions.

The organization started in March 1992 when NGO representatives wanted to design effective information and communications structures to facilitate the flow of information about development. They wanted this information to come from affected populations to the relevant policymakers in order to promote involvement of civil-society groups in decision making about issues related to sustainable development.

Registered in Kenya, EcoNews operates on a subregional level, working with NGOs and community-based organizations in Kenya, Tanzania, Uganda, Djibouti, Eritrea, Ethiopia, Somalia and Sudan.

The Community Media program's primary objective is to develop community managed and controlled communications and information structures among civil-society groups in eastern and southern Africa in order to enhance their ability to organize themselves and participate effectively in policymaking.

[4]*Excerpted from a case study written by Alfonso Gumucio Dagron based on information supplied by Wagaki Mwangi and Lynne Muthoni Wanyeki of EcoNews.*

This program is founded on the premise that media owned, controlled and produced by, for and about local communities is essential to the establishment of forums to critically examine development concerns, including governance and human rights issues—as well as preservation of indigenous cultures and knowledge.

The Community Media program has three components:

- Advocacy, through the Kenya Community Media Network (KCOMNET): This is a forum for media professionals interested in promoting the growth of community communications in Kenya. They advocate for establishment of a regulatory framework that enhances the community media sector, including the pervasiveness of community broadcasting and the use of new information and communication technologies.

- The East African Pilot Project: Started in August 1993, this project helps three communities, located in remote villages without access to telephones or grid electricity, to set up horizontal communication structures which will enable them to share their stories with people around the world.

- Facilitating the work of the steering committee of the Community Media Network for Eastern and Southern Africa (COMNESA). COMNESA is a regional platform for community media practitioners whose mission is to establish a movement of community media practitioners in the region.

The program also provides technical and fund-raising support to community groups in the region working to establish community radio stations and Internet connectivity.

EcoNews' total annual budget, which funds the Community Media program and four others, is U.S. $400,000.

Púlsar: Strengthening Community Radio with E-Communications[5]
Agencia Informativa Púlsar/AMARC

Púlsar was started by AMARC (Association of Community Radio Broadcasters) in March 1996 to provide independent and community radio stations in Latin America with local news stories, public-service advertisements and other information useful to civil society. It was the first initiative of its kind in Latin America. From 38 subscribers, Púlsar has grown to more than 1,000 subscribers in two years. Most are radio stations, but some are NGOs and individuals who use the information provided for different purposes: news, teaching and political analysis, for example. All services are provided free of charge.

From the beginning Púlsar has sought to:

1. Improve the programming, establish credibility and increase the impact of independent and community radio in Latin America.

2. Contribute to modernizing and upgrading the technology of independent and community radio stations.

3. Ensure the spread of better information and knowledge of regional and global issues; promote topics related to democratic development, regional integration, peace and human rights, and the right to communicate.

4. Promote pluralism and participation at the local, national and regional levels, giving priority to those sectors which are often excluded.

Púlsar began by producing a daily bulletin of 12-to-15 stories, five days per week. Within a year it had added a

---

[5]*Excerpted from a case study written by Alfonso Gumucio Dagron and based on information supplied by Bruce Girard, Púlsar's former director, and Sophie Ly, secretary-general of AMARC.*

monthly Communicado and by the end of 1998 the following specialized services:

- *El Línea,* news stories edited and distributed throughout the day Monday through Friday;
- *Compendio,* a collection of all the news stories produced during the day, transmitted at the end of each day;
- *Ciberbrujas,* produced in collaboration with the Bolivian NGO REDADA, this weekly service features news and information about Latin American women;
- *Ñuqanchik,* a daily news service in Quechua, the main native language of the Andean region which is spoken by nearly 8 million people;
- *Audio,* a daily service of audio clips from 15-to-60 seconds that contain voices from those in the news, or socially-oriented ads.

Púlsar uses the Internet (e-mail) to distribute news about Latin America and for Latin Americans to community radio stations. It trains local correspondents and stations to use new technology.

Because very few community radio stations used e-mail or the Internet when the initiative began in 1996, the promotion of new technologies became one of Púlsar's main strategies. They designed and sent a diskette, Viaje Virtual, which explains the advantages of information technology, to 350 radio stations. Today Púlsar's Web site attracts thousands of visitors each month (www.amarc.org/pulsar).

AMARC represents thousands of community radio stations worldwide and is committed to strengthening community radio.

APPENDIX II
1997 BELLAGIO CONFERENCE HIGHLIGHTS AND DECLARATION OF PRINCIPLES

Vision of Communication for Social Change

We recognize that the practice and systems of communications have the power to transform lives, and to influence the behavior of organizations, institutions, communities and nations. We also believe that for too long the processes and systems of communications have been concentrated within the power of too few in industrialized countries who use such power to homogenize cultures and ideologies. Recognizing this, and that communication systems and processes are not easily accessible to all the world's people, we, the following, joined together to propose a vision of communications for the 21st century that animates our collective commitment to positive social change.

This vision is shaped by the following principles:

I. Every voice has the right to be heard and should have the means to be heard.

II. Communications systems and technology must, therefore, be affordable, accessible to all.

III. To work best, the process of communication must allow a free flow from many to many, rather than from one to many.

IV. Communities must play an essential role in finding their own communications solutions and developing their own communications strategies.

We believe that unmediated communication processes, in which all of us may communicate freely, directly and horizontally with one another, will endow each of us with a greater sense of our own possibilities, enrich our cultures through direct contact with other cultures, create a conversation without limits in which each voice may be heard equally, and from which may evolve enlightened societies that value tolerance, self-determination and active participation.

We believe in the power of strong, vivid and personal images to transform consciousness. And we believe that the images and stories that define and shape a group, a community or a people are primarily theirs alone to make.

For we believe that the cultures of the world need not be subsumed by those cultures of industrialized nations which dominate control of channels of communications.

We believe that ideas with the power to enhance our lives are arising from voices too long excluded from the larger human discourse. These are too often the voices of people from the edges of the world, from the margins of society. They may own neither presses nor broadcasting towers, but they do have the capability of taking responsibility for their futures. We've seen how many previously marginalized people, given the opportunity, can create solutions for complex world problems, and may, in fact, well possess the energy and vision that will help ensure the future for all of us.

We believe that communication is essential for strengthening cultural identity and human values, encouraging further world development, allowing people in communities throughout the world to participate in their own governance, to organize, and to shape our future world.

Moved to action by these principles, we have agreed to work together toward free and open access of all people to the methods, means and tools of communication, to reach out to communities around the world for their ideas and their strength, and to embrace and promote new understanding and new knowledge from wherever it might arise.

Having traveled from 12 countries in late April of 1997 to meet together in Bellagio, Italy, we are:

- Alan Alda, actor/ writer/ director, New York, N.Y., U.S.A.
- Marlene Arnold, The Leadership Institute, Millersville, Pa., U.S.A.
- Michael Backes, Rocket Science Games, Sherman Oaks, Calif., U.S.A.
- Oguz Baburoglu, Sabanci University, Istanbul, Turkey
- John Perry Barlow, Electronic Frontier Foundation, Pinedale, Wyo., U.S.A.
- James Deane, Panos Institute, London, England
- George Gerbner, Temple University, Philadelphia, Pa., U.S.A.
- Sushmita Ghosh, Ashoka: Innovators for the Public, Calcutta, India
- Julie Gipwola, Radio Uganda, Kampala, Uganda
- Denise Gray-Felder, The Rockefeller Foundation, New York, N.Y., U.S.A.
- Alfonso Gumucio, Guatemala City, Guatemala (formerly Port-au-Prince, Haiti)
- Myoung Joon Kim, Videazimut, Seoul, Korea[*]
- Jim Lowenthal,[+] Morocco Trade and Development Services, Rabat-Agdal, Morocco
- Susan Mach, LS Mach Creative Services, Kearny, N. J., U.S.A.
- Matthew Moonieya, Moonieya & Associates, East London, South Africa
- Jenny Richards, TVE International, London, England
- Marcia Sharp, Millenium Communications, Inc., Washington, D.C., U.S.A.
- Nadya Seryakova, New Perspectives Foundation, Moscow, Russia[*]

[*] *Translation by Hye-June Park and Edward Kushelov.*

[+]*Dedicated to our friend and colleague Jim Lowenthal who died in the summer of 1998.*

- Julie Su, Asian Pacific American Legal Center, Los Angeles, Calif., U.S.A.
- Adelaida Trujillo, Citurna Films, Bogota, Colombia
- Galina Venediktova, Women, Law & Development International, Arlington, Va., (Currently U.S.A.; native of Russia)
- Muhammad Yunus, Grameen Bank, Dhaka, Bangladesh

APPENDIX III
Cape Town Participants 1998:
- Fackson Banda, Communications and Social Justice, Christian Council of Zambia, Lusaka, Zambia
- Brian Byrd, The Rockefeller Foundation, New York, N.Y., U.S.A.
- Dayna Cunningham, The Rockefeller Foundation, New York, N.Y., U.S.A.
- James Deane, Panos Institute, London, England
- Jean Fairbairn, Open Society Foundation for South Africa, Cape Town, South Africa
- Warren Feek, The Communication Initiative, Victoria, British Columbia
- Judi Fortuin Nwokedi, Advocacy Initiatives, Johannesburg, South Africa
- George Gerbner, Bell Atlantic Professor of Telecommunication, Temple University; dean emeritus, University of Pennsylvania, Philadelphia, Pa., U.S.A.
- Sushmita Ghosh, ASHOKA: Innovators for the Public Interest, Calcutta, India
- Julie Gipwola, Coordinator, AIDS Control Program (ACP), Radio Uganda/Uganda Dept. of Information, Kampala, Uganda
- Denise Gray-Felder, The Rockefeller Foundation, New York, N.Y., U.S.A.
- Zane Ibrahim, Bush Radio, Cape Town, South Africa
- Garth Japhet, Soul City, Johannesburg, South Africa

- Myoung Joon Kim, Labor News Productions, Videazimut, Seoul, Korea
- Freddy Kodio, PSI–Chad, Masocot Project, N'djamena, Chad
- Evelyn Lieberman, Voice of America, Washington, D.C., U.S.A.
- Sophie Ly, AMARC (Association for Community Radio Broadcasters), Montreal, Quebec
- Kumi Naidoo, Civicus: World Alliance for Citizen Participation, Washington, D.C., U.S.A.
- Karen Polk, The Rockefeller Foundation, New York, N.Y., U.S.A.
- Hu Jia-Rong, Rural Women Knowing All Magazine, Beijing, China
- Sukulu Rupeni, ACT Coordinator, FSP Fiji, Suva, Fiji
- P. Sainath, Bandra Reclamation, Mumbai, India
- Marcia Sharp, Millenium Communications Group Inc., Washington, D.C., U.S.A.
- George Soule, The Rockefeller Foundation, New York, N.Y., U.S.A.
- Fatoumata Sow, Association pour les Femmes et la Communication Alternative - Altercom, Dakar, Senegal
- Nazneen Sultana, Grameen Communications, Grameen Bank Bhaban, Dhaka, Bangladesh
- Adelaida Trujillo, Citurna Film and Video Productions, Bogota, Colombia
- Victoria Vrana, Millennium Communications Group Inc., Washington, D.C., U.S.A.
- Lynne Muthoni Wanyeki, EcoNews, Nairobi, Kenya
- Maggie Williams, Paris, France